Further Ess
Eastern Initiation

Early Syrian Baptismal Liturgy

Paul F. Bradshaw

Emeritus Professor of Liturgy, University of Notre Dame, USA

Juliette Day

University Lecturer in Church History,
Faculty of Theology, University of Helsinki, Finland

Contents

Cover image: Basilica church with towers, Eastern Mediterranean from second half of the 5th century. Louvre Museum, Paris. Photograph: Robin Jensen used with permission.

© Paul Bradshaw and Juliette Day 2014

ISSN: 0951-2667

ISBN: 978-1-84825-626-2

Editorial Note

The title of this Study has an echo from Alcuin/GROW Joint Liturgical Study 8 (Grove Books, Bramcote, 1988). This was edited by Paul Bradshaw under the title *Essays in Early Eastern Initiation* and presented three essays:

'Baptismal Practice in the Alexandrian Tradition, Eastern or Western?' by Paul F. Bradshaw
'Reconciling Cyril and Egeria on the Catechetical Process in Fourth-Century Jerusalem' by Maxwell E. Johnson
'The Structure of the Syrian Baptismal Liturgy' by Ruth A. Meyers

The 26 years which have elapsed since this symposium was published have seen vast further research and study brought to bear upon the early Eastern rites, as both text and footnotes of the two present essays testify. So the echo remains a happy echo, not a claim that the present essays are written in unbroken continuity with those of 1988.

'Juliette Day's essay reproduces an earlier work of hers published by De Gruyter of Berlin and Boston, MA, and is included here by kind permission of De Gruyter..

1

Early Patterns of Christian Initiation in Syria

Paul F. Bradshaw

The Winkler thesis

Gabriele Winkler's 1978 article, 'The Original Meaning of the Pre-baptismal Anointing and its Implications',[1] brought about a profound transformation in the understanding of early Syrian baptismal practice and continues to be cited as the standard work in nearly every study of the subject down to the present day. In it she argued forcefully that, contrary to the conclusions of earlier scholarship, the original Syrian practice 'knew only one pre-baptismal anointing, namely, the pouring of oil over the head, and that only at a later period in history was the whole body anointed'. She concluded that in the oldest stratum of the tradition:

> Christian baptism is shaped after Christ's baptism in the Jordan. As Jesus had received the anointing through the divine presence in the appearance of a dove, and was invested as the Messiah, so in Christian baptism every candidate is anointed and, in connection

---

[1] *Worship* 52 (1978), pp. 24–45, reprinted in Maxwell E. Johnson (ed.), *Living Water, Sealing Spirit: Readings on Christian Initiation* (Liturgical Press, Collegeville, 1995), pp. 58–81.

with this anointing, the gift of the Spirit is conferred. Therefore the main theme of this pre-baptismal anointing is the entry into the eschatological kingship of the Messiah, being in the true sense of the word assimilated to the Messiah–King through this anointing.[2]

This, she believed, explained why at first oil was poured only over the head (this was the custom at the anointing of the kings of Israel); why the coming of the Spirit was associated with it (the Spirit of the Lord came over the newly nominated king); and why the anointing and not the immersion in water was regarded as the central feature of baptism in the early Syrian sources (this was the only visible gesture for what was held to be the central event at Christ's baptism – his revelation as the Messiah–King through the descent of the Spirit).

Winkler argued that the subsequent introduction of an anointing of the whole body led to the loss of its original impact and its reinterpretation as a cathartic and apotropaic ritual along the Greek-speaking coastline of the Mediterranean, in contrast to East Syria and Armenia. The conferring of the Spirit together with the themes of royal and sacerdotal anointing were transferred first to the immersion itself in the thought of John Chrysostom, and then to a newly introduced post-baptismal unction at Jerusalem in the late fourth century. This change also led to the reinterpretation of the rite as a death/resurrection event, in accordance with Romans 6, rather than a birth event, in accordance with John 3.

She rejected the theory of Edward Ratcliff, that the eventual adoption of a post-baptismal anointing in all Eastern rites was due to the influence of Jerusalem, as well as the hypothesis of Bernard Botte, that it was the result of the practice of anointing heretics on their return to orthodoxy. She claimed instead that it happened because of the inner change of dynamics within the ritual itself. Once baptism moved away from its original essence, being the mimesis of the event at the Jordan, and shifted at the same time toward a cathartic principle, it was inevitable that all rites

---

[2] *Ibid*, p. 36.

that preceded baptism proper became subordinated to a process of thorough cleansing. The catharsis slowly became an indispensable condition for the coming of the Spirit. Consequently, only after intensive purification and the washing away of sins could the Spirit enter the heart of the baptized.[3]

Two successive stages or parallel traditions?

In the years that have passed since Winkler's article first appeared, scholarship surrounding early Christian liturgical practice has undergone a number of changes and developments, some of which suggest that her conclusions now need to be nuanced. As a result of the influence of what one leading scholar has described as a 'neo-skeptic school of paleo-liturgiologists', the idea of the existence of an original single archetypical rite that gradually evolved into one or more different forms has begun to be seriously questioned with regard to both the eucharist and also other liturgical rites. Thus, what Winkler interpreted as successive stages of the evolution of the pre-baptismal anointing – from the head alone associated with the Spirit to the whole body associated with protection and healing – may instead have been two parallel co-existent traditions from different regions of Syria.

The only very early evidence for a pre-baptismal anointing of the head alone occurs in the *Acts of Judas Thomas*. Although this work is believed to have been originally written in Syriac in the early third century, scholars are generally of the opinion that the extant Syriac version is later than the extant Greek version and has undergone some theological re-interpretation.[4] Certainly, there are significant differences between the two. In the Syriac version two stories about baptisms, in chapters 25—7 and 132—3, describe an anointing of the head alone, which is associated with the Messiah and has no blessing prayer preceding it. Two other stories, in chapters 121 and 156–8, describe an anointing of both the head and the whole body, which

---

[3] *Ibid.*, p. 42, n. 63.

[4] See Harold W. Attridge, 'The Original Language of the *Acts of Thomas*' in Harold W. Attridge, John J. Collins, and Thomas H. Tobin (eds), *Of Scribes and Scrolls* (University of America Press, Lanham, MD, 1990), pp. 241–50; Jan N. Bremmer, 'The *Acts of Thomas*: Place, Date and Women' in *idem* (ed.), *The Apocryphal Acts of Thomas* (Peeters, Louvain, 2001), pp. 74–90.

is focused on the theme of healing and includes a prayer for the blessing of the oil beforehand. However, in the Greek version of chapters 25—27 Thomas not only pours oil on the heads of the candidates, as in the Syriac version, but is also said to have then 'anointed and chrismated them', and there is no explicit mention of baptism afterwards. On the other hand, the story in chapter 121 lacks mention of an anointing of the body in addition to that of the head.[5]

These variations imply that the Syriac accounts are not based on the extant Greek text, but rather that we are dealing with two parallel modifications of the presumed missing Syriac original. Although it might be argued that the Syriac version of the story in chapter 121 could have added the anointing of the body to the anointing of the head in the Greek version, that is obviously not the case with the additions made in the Greek to the anointing of the head alone in chapters 25—27. The suggestion by A. F. J. Klijn, that the translator here had in mind a post-baptismal chrismation, especially as early in chapter 25 baptism and anointing are mentioned in that order, appears to have merit.[6] Above all, the fact that the stories in chapters 132—33 and 156—58 describe an anointing of the head alone and of both head and body respectively in both the Greek and Syriac versions points to both patterns of pre-baptismal anointing being known to the compiler of the earliest text.

Furthermore, the practice of anointing of the head was not superseded everywhere by an anointing of head and body. Sebastian Brock has drawn attention to a number of later Syrian liturgical texts where an anointing of the head alone occurs, including one tenth-century manuscript in particular (BM Add. 14493, ff. 165—170), although the accompanying formula obviously has been influenced by rites where there was also an anointing of the head and body.[7] He also published a translation of a

---

[5] For a convenient English translation of extracts from all these texts, see E. C. Whitaker, *Documents of the Baptismal Liturgy*, 3rd edn ed. Maxwell E. Johnson (Alcuin Club Collections 79, SPCK, London, 2003), pp. 16–21.

[6] A. F. J. Klijn, *The Acts of Thomas: Introduction, Text, Commentary* (Brill, Leiden, 1962), pp. 55–56.

[7] Sebastian Brock, 'Studies in the Early History of the Syrian Orthodox Baptismal Liturgy' in *Journal of Theological Studies* 23 (1972), pp. 16–64, here at 21, 30 (especially n. 2), 39.

Syrian baptismal commentary, the oldest recension of which mentions only a pre-baptismal anointing of the head and which he dated to the early fifth century.[8] The more likely explanation therefore seems to be that the two distinct practices with their differing interpretations of the meaning of the action co-existed with one another in different parts of Syria. Indeed, Winkler herself accepted the existence of an element of regional variation when she acknowledged that 'along the Greek-speaking coastline of the Mediterranean, in contrast to East Syria and Armenia, the preparatory rites of baptism developed into one of the most evolved and important parts of the whole baptismal liturgy'.[9]

The Didascalia Apostolorum

In addition to the two instances of whole body anointing that occur in the *Acts of Thomas*, the practice is also assumed in the *Didascalia Apostolorum*. This Syrian church order was formerly regarded as the work of a single compiler in the first half of the third century but has been convincingly shown by Alistair Stewart-Sykes to be a composite work containing material from the second through to the fourth century.[10] Therefore, although we shall for convenience continue to speak of its 'compiler', that is not to deny that several hands were involved in the compilation of this church order. What is vital, however, is to take account of the particular context in which the reference to whole body anointing at baptism occurs. It is not in a section of detailed instructions about baptism in general, but in one concerned with the desirability for women to minister in certain situations,[11] and especially in the pre-baptismal anointing of female candidates for baptism because 'it is not right that a

---

[8] Sebastian Brock, 'Some Early Syrian Baptismal Commentaries' in *Orientalia Christiana Periodica* 46 (1980), pp. 20–61.

[9] Winkler, 'The Original Meaning of the Pre-baptismal Anointing and its Implications', p. 39.

[10] Alistair Stewart-Sykes, *The Didascalia Apostolorum: An English Version with Introduction and Annotation* (Brepols, Turnhout, 2009).

[11] *Didascalia* 3.12. The specific mention of women *deacons* here appears to be a later addition to an older core of the material that simply spoke of women. See Paul F. Bradshaw, 'Women and Baptism in the *Didascalia Apostolorum*' in *Journal of Early Christian Studies* 20 (2012), pp. 641–645.

woman should be seen by a man' – thus indicating that the anointing was of the whole body. The compiler is therefore simply proposing a solution to the specific problem of what should be done when females are baptized, and what is recommended is that the candidate's head should be anointed by the bishop but the rest of her body by a woman in order to preserve decorum. Exactly the same practice is adopted in the two instances of whole body anointing in the *Acts of Thomas*, where again the candidates were female in both cases: the candidate's head was anointed by the male apostle and the rest of her body by a woman.

Since the *Didascalia*, like other ancient sources, is insistent that the immersion itself must be performed by a man even in the case of women candidates, it may be wondered how the women's bodies could avoid being seen by male eyes at that stage. Although the *Didascalia* itself does not allude to any explanation for this situation, in both instances in the *Acts of Thomas* the females put on some sort of linen undergarment after their bodies have been anointed by other women, and they presumably continued to wear this during the immersion. Thus, the assumption often made that both men and women were baptized naked in early Christian practice may not have held true everywhere, and especially not in Syria, where there may have been a greater concern for female modesty than in other parts of the ancient world. Laurie Guy has argued that even in the case of men, 'naked' may only have meant removing the outer garments, although Robin Jensen has suggested that the widespread baptismal iconography depicting Christ as nude at his baptism makes it 'difficult to imagine candidates wearing clothes (or even simple undergarments) directly below an image of the immersion of their naked Saviour'.[12]

It was, however, the division of the act of anointing into two parts that encouraged Winkler to believe that head and body anointing must have

---

[12] Laurie Guy, '"Naked" Baptism in the Early Church: The Rhetoric and the Reality' in *Journal of Religious History* 27 (2003), pp. 133–142; Robin M. Jensen, *Baptismal Imagery in Early Christianity* (Baker Academic, Grand Rapids, 2012), p. 160.

developed out of a head only anointing, and her supposition appeared to be strengthened by the fact that the compiler of the *Didascalia* then attributes a separate significance to the anointing of the head: 'As in ancient times the priests and kings of Israel were anointed, so you should do the same, anointing the head, with a laying on of a hand, of those who come to baptism.'[13] But that is to assume that the same division between the anointing of the head and the anointing of the rest of the body was also made in the case of male candidates and was not simply a practical solution for the initiation of women, in respect of which the compiler had searched the scriptures in order to produce a precedent for separating that part of the anointing. As Charles Whitaker observed many years ago, the compiler was 'not necessarily saying anything about the purpose or meaning of the rite'.[14]

Certainly, in the *Acts of Thomas* no special interpretation is given to the anointing of the head as distinct from the anointing the rest of the body, but the whole action appears to be associated with the concept of healing according to the prayers of blessing over the oil that accompany it. Moreover, in one of the two instances (that in Chapter 157) a man is also baptized, and the apostle himself anoints both his head and his body. Even in the fourth century, when we do begin to see a temporal separation of the anointing of the head from the anointing of the rest of the body in the case of male candidates too, the same minister performs both actions and no separate theological rationale is given for the anointing of the head. Thus, in two of his baptismal homilies John Chrysostom refers to an anointing of the head apparently taking place on an earlier day than the anointing of the rest of the body (although he is not very explicit about this separation), but both are associated primarily with protection from evil, and both appear to

---

[13] *Didascalia* 3.12.2–3; English translation from Stewart-Sykes, *The Didascalia Apostolorum*, p. 193.

[14] E. C. Whitaker, 'Unction in the Syrian Baptismal Rite' in *Church Quarterly Review* 162 (1961), pp. 176–187, here at p. 181.

be performed by the bishop. He anoints the forehead with the sign of the cross[15] accompanied by a Trinitarian formula in order to 'hold in check all the frenzy of the Evil One' and 'make the devil turn away his eyes', and subsequently anoints the body to 'armour all your limbs and make them invulnerable to any weapons the Enemy may hurl'.[16] Later writers do add other interpretations – for example, Theodore of Mopsuestia describes the two anointings as being performed by different ministers and depicts the unction of the forehead as the reception of the identification mark of a sheep or soldier of Christ and that of the body as symbolizing the garment of immortality that will be received through baptism[17] – but in no instance is the anointing of the forehead seen as a royal or priestly unction when an anointing of the whole body follows.

The instances that are cited by Winkler where this imagery is used are all in relation to rites where there is an anointing of the head alone: the Armenian rite with its prayer linking 1 Peter 2.9 to the anointing of priests, kings and prophets; the presence of similar imagery in the Armenian *Teaching of St Gregory*; and a hymn of Ephrem the Syrian that mentions the anointing of priests and kings in relation to the gift of the Spirit in baptismal anointing.[18] It can certainly be argued, as Winkler does, that these are all examples of what was once the universal Syrian understanding of an original pre-baptismal anointing of the head alone, which disappeared in the West Syrian tradition when the action was converted into a head and whole body anointing and re-interpreted.

---

[15] As Winkler notes ('The Original Meaning of the Prebaptismal Anointing and its Implications', p. 36, n. 30), the anointing of the forehead with the sign of the cross appears to be a later development, as the older sources speak of pouring or casting the oil on the head.

[16] See Whitaker, *Documents of the Baptismal Liturgy*, p. 43 (for Papadopoulos-Kerameus 3:27), pp. 45–46 (for Stavronikita 2:22–4). For a fuller exposition of Chrysostom's baptismal theology, see Mark Roosien, 'Putting on Christ: Metaphor and Martyrdom in John Chrysostom's *Baptismal Instructions*' in *Studia Liturgica* 43 (2013), pp. 54–67.

[17] Theodore of Mopsuestia, *Baptismal Homilies* 2.17–20; 3.8; English translation in Whitaker, *Documents of the Baptismal Liturgy*, pp. 48–49.

[18] Winkler, 'The Original Meaning of the Pre-baptismal Anointing and its Implications', pp. 32–33.

The question to be asked, however, is how likely it is that there was such a complete disappearance and transformation that left virtually no trace. Is not the evidence better understood by the supposition that there never was a single universal practice and theology, but rather two parallel traditions, both employing oil but in quite distinct ways and with quite different understandings? One tradition would have included an anointing of the whole head and body for healing and protection in preparation for baptism and the gift of the Spirit in the water, and the other an anointing of the head alone, understood as the conferral of the Spirit before the immersion and incorporating the typology of the anointing of kings and priests in the Old Testament.

Several patterns?

A few scholars have gone further and suggested that more than two patterns of initiation co-existed in Syria.[19] Clearly, at one time there were communities that practised immersion in water without any accompanying anointings at all. Not only is this what is prescribed in the oldest extant Syrian church order, the *Didache* – although a few scholars have, improbably, tried to infer the presence of an anointing there because of the appearance of a prayer over ointment in the later Coptic version of the text[20] – but it has been thought by some that the continuing existence of this pattern at a later date may be signalled by another initiation story in the *Acts of Thomas* (Chapter 49), that of a woman possessed by a devil, where water alone is mentioned in the Syriac version.[21]

Alastair Logan, however, has argued that there was also a further pattern that involved anointing after the immersion rather than before

---

[19] See in particular Bryan D. Spinks, 'Baptismal Patterns in Early Syria: Another Reading', in Maxwell E. Johnson and L. Edward Phillips (eds), *Studia Liturgica Diversa: Essays in Honor of Paul F. Bradshaw* (Pastoral Press, Portland, OR, 2004), pp. 45–52. But for a cautious response, see Maxwell E. Johnson, *The Rites of Christian Initiation: Their Evolution and Interpretation*, 2nd edn (Liturgical Press, Collegeville, 2004), pp. 78–82.

[20] See J. Ysebaert, 'The So-called Coptic Ointment Prayer of Didache 10.8 Once More' in *Vigiliae Christianae* 56 (2002), pp. 1–10.

[21] *Acts of Thomas* 49 (Whitaker, *Documents of the Baptismal Liturgy*, p. 17).

it. He based this on his interpretation of certain ambiguous texts circulating in Gnostic circles as reflecting a post-baptismal anointing,[22] and on the supposition that they would have been paralleled by a similar practice in more orthodox Christian groups. While this cannot be ruled out as a possibility, he is unable to adduce any convincing testimony that it actually was so. All the other evidence he cites is of an anointing in connection with baptism, but it says nothing about its position within the rite.[23]

On the other hand, the presence of a post-baptismal unction in the fourth-century rites of Jerusalem and of Egypt, in which various parts of the body rather than the head were anointed (though not exactly the same parts in each case),[24] does not seem a natural choice to express the descent of the Spirit. Nor does it seem to be the result of an 'inner change of dynamics within the ritual itself', in which the rites were no longer shaped after the Jordan event but followed Paul's doctrine of dying and rising with Christ, and so necessitated the gift of the Spirit to come after the immersion, as Winkler concluded.[25] Moreover, as Juliette Day has observed, none of the explanations given in the *Mystagogical Catecheses* for each place being anointed is explicitly Christological or pneumatological,[26] and this suggests the likelihood that the combination of this anointing with the bestowal of the Spirit is a secondary development. Thus, it is certainly possible that the idea of adding a post-baptismal unction may have percolated from a practice of anointing the

---

[22] Alastair Logan, 'The Mystery of the Five Seals: Gnostic Initiation Reconsidered' in *Vigiliae Christianae* 51 (1997), pp. 188–206.

[23] Alastair Logan, 'Post-Baptismal Chrismation in Syria: The Evidence of Ignatius, the *Didache* and the *Apostolic Constitutions*' in *Journal of Theological Studies* 49 (1998), pp. 92–108. But see Simon Jones, 'Womb of the Spirit: The Liturgical Implications of the Doctrine of the Spirit for the Syrian Baptismal Tradition' (Ph.D. thesis, Cambridge University, 1999), pp. 54–56, who argues for a post-baptismal imposition of hands in the *Didascalia*.

[24] At Jerusalem: the forehead, ears, nostrils, and chest (*Mystagogical Catecheses* 3.4; English translation in E. J. Yarnold, *The Awe-Inspiring Rites of Initiation*, 2nd edn (T & T Clark, Edinburgh/ Liturgical Press, Collegeville, 1994), pp. 83–84); in Egypt, according to the *Canons of Hippolytus*: the forehead, mouth and chest (Whitaker, *Documents of the Baptismal Liturgy*, p. 131). Neither included the eyes in later Eastern traditions.

[25] Winkler, 'The Original Meaning of the Prebaptismal Anointing and its Implications', pp. 39–42.

[26] Juliette Day, *The Baptismal Liturgy of Jerusalem* (Ashgate, Aldershot, 2007), p. 111.

five senses in Christian Gnostic circles into more mainstream usage.[27]

Christian baptism and the baptism of Jesus

Winkler asserted that 'in the oldest Syriac documents Christian baptism is shaped after Christ's baptism in the Jordan', and 'this concept of shaping the baptismal liturgy after what had happened at the Jordan certainly represents the oldest and most powerful stratum in Syria.'[28] For this she is principally reliant upon the *Didascalia Apostolorum* and the Armenian *Teaching of St Gregory*, as the baptismal stories in the *Acts of Thomas* certainly do not make any such connection explicit. The compiler of the *Didascalia* appears to connect Christian baptism with the baptism of Jesus, not in the section about women but elsewhere in a section about the honour due to the bishop, where he says: 'in baptism, through the imposition of the bishop's hand, the Lord bore witness of each of you, as his holy voice was heard, saying: "You are my son, this day I have begotten you."'[29] It is this quotation from Psalm 2.7, which appears as a variant reading to, 'You are my beloved Son; with you I am well pleased', at the baptism of Jesus in Luke 3.22, that suggests that the baptism of Jesus may be in the compiler's mind here. The variant is found in the Codex Bezae and seven Old Latin texts of the New Testament as well as being cited by a number of patristic authors, including Justin Martyr in his account of the baptism of Jesus in the *Dialogue with Trypho* (chapter 88). According to Epiphanius, the two readings were combined in the Ebionite Gospel.[30]

Winkler understood the reference to the imposition of the hand here as being to the act of anointing the head,[31] as a laying on of the hand

---

[27] This possibility had also been suggested long ago by Geoffrey Lampe, *The Seal of the Spirit*, 2nd edn (SPCK, London, 1967), p. 127.

[28] Winkler, 'The Original Meaning of the Prebaptismal Anointing and its Implications', pp. 36–37.

[29] *Didascalia* 2.33.3; English translation from Stewart-Sykes, *The Didascalia Apostolorum*, p. 155.

[30] Epiphanius, *Adversus Haereses* 30.13. For a discussion of the possibility that the variant might in fact be the original reading of the text, see Kilian McDonnell, *The Baptism of Jesus in the Jordan* (Liturgical Press, Collegeville, 1996), pp. 85ff..

[31] Winkler, 'The Original Meaning of the Prebaptismal Anointing and its Implications', p. 36.

for that purpose is explicitly mentioned in the section on women and baptism. Stewart-Sykes, however, has suggested that the reference is rather to the placing of the bishop's hand on the baptizand's head in order to push him/her under the water in the act of immersion, and he refers to *Acta Iohannis* 40, where this action is described: 'The holy man drew near and placed his hand on the head of the procurator and dipped him....'[32] To this may be added the words of John Chrysostom in one of his baptismal homilies:

> After this anointing he takes you down into the sacred waters.... Then by the words of the priest and by his hand the presence of the Holy Spirit flies down upon you.... As the priest pronounced the words, 'N. is baptized in the name of the Father and of the Son and of the Holy Spirit', he plunges your head into the water and lifts it up again three times, by this sacred rite preparing you to receive the descent of the Holy Spirit. For the priest is not the only one who touches your head. Christ also touches it with his right hand....[33]

Winkler also believed the words quoted from Psalm 2.7 were a liturgical formula that was said by the bishop while imposing his hand, following the claim to this effect made by E. C. Ratcliff. Even Ratcliff admitted, however, that the use of the formula appears to have been confined to the Didascaliast's own Greek-speaking area. There is no trace of it in the Syriac-speaking areas represented by the *Acts of Thomas* and the *History of John*. Further, there is no evidence to show that the formula continued in use in the Antiochene area beyond the Didascaliast's time.[34]

---

[32] Stewart-Sykes, *The Didascalia Apostolorum*, p. 155, n. 35.

[33] Stavronikita 2.25–26, in Whitaker, *Documents of the Baptismal Liturgy*, 46. See also Theodore of Mopsuestia, *Baptismal Homily* 3.14, 18–19; English translation, *ibid.*, p. 50.

[34] E. C. Ratcliff, 'The Old Syrian Baptismal Tradition and its Resettlement under the influence of Jerusalem in the Fourth Century' in *Studies in Church History* 2 (1965) pp. 19–37, here at 24. The possibility that the words were a formula said at the anointing was cautiously endorsed by Johnson, *The Rites of Christian Initiation*, p. 54.

One may well then wonder whether it ever was such a formula at all. We have seen earlier that the compiler seems to have quarried the Old Testament for a text to provide a precedent for the anointing of the head. Might not this be just another such example, intended metaphorically rather than literally?

What does seem sure is that the alleged formula would not have accompanied the immersion because 'the invocation of the divine names' is said have been pronounced during that action (*Didascalia* 3.12.3). This appears to be a reference to a Trinitarian formula. The *Didache* in its directions concerning the conferral of baptism appears to prescribe just such a formula: 'Baptize in the name of the Father and of the Son and of the Holy Spirit.'[35] While some have suggested that this is a later expansion of a text that originally spoke only of baptizing 'in the name of the Lord', as in *Didache* 9.5,[36] and others have questioned whether it was intended as an actual spoken formula at all,[37] most scholars have concluded that it was widely used from early times in Syria because the same formula appears in the baptismal stories in the *Acts of Thomas* and also in fourth-century sources (although in the passive rather than the active, 'N. is baptized in the name…').[38]

Whatever the case, the Psalm quotation is not sufficient to demonstrate that the rite itself was modelled on the baptism of Jesus. In Luke and the other synoptic gospel accounts of the baptism of Jesus the Holy Spirit descends and the heavenly voice speaks only after he has come up out of the water. If the laying on of hands and the formula accompanied the pre-baptismal anointing, as Winkler supposed, then the ritual sequence would have been quite different from that in the gospels. Even if the reference is instead to the bishop's laying on of hands at the immersion,

---

[35] *Didache* 7; English translation in Whitaker, *Documents of the Baptismal Liturgy*, p. 2.

[36] See Willy Rordorf, 'Baptism according to the Didache', in Jonathan A. Draper (ed.), *The Didache in Modern Research* (Brill, Leiden, 1996), pp. 212–222, here at 217; Arthur Vööbus, *Liturgical Traditions in the Didache* (Estonian Theological Society in Exile, Stockholm, 1968), pp. 36–39.

[37] See, for example, Johnson, *The Rites of Christian Initiation*, pp. 45–46.

[38] See, for example, John Chrysostom, *Baptismal Homily*, Stavronikita 2.26, in Whitaker, *Documents of the Baptismal Liturgy*, p. 46.

it still would not have been parallel to those accounts. And if we were to go so far as to concede that the anointing of the head had originally signified the descent of the Spirit on the baptizands, as Winkler argued, then the sequence would have been even further removed from that of the baptism of Jesus. The compiler of the *Didascalia* certainly associated Christian baptism with the baptism of Jesus – the earliest author explicitly to do so – but it would be going too far to say that the rite was actually modelled on that event.[39] Maxwell Johnson is thus nearer the truth when he defends Winkler's claim as being based 'not on *sequence* as much as on ritual *signification*'.[40]

The Holy Spirit and Baptism

Bryan Spinks suggests that a better paradigm for this Syrian pattern 'might be the incarnation of Jesus and then his baptism, where the messianic Spirit hovers at conception to bring forth new birth'.[41] The compiler of the *Didascalia* certainly interpreted baptism not only as conveying forgiveness of sins[42] but also as bestowing new birth. Within a list of things that bishops do, for which they should be honoured, are included 'who have begotten you anew through water, who filled you with the Holy Spirit' (2.33.2). Earlier in the list is a sentence that, though somewhat obscure, seems to make the same point: the bishops are 'those through whom you became a son of God, and [through] the right hand, [they became] your mother'.[43] With regard to the Holy Spirit, however, the paradigm does not seem to work so well. As we have seen, Winkler believed that the compiler understood the Spirit to be conferred through

---

[39] This challenge to Winkler had already been made by Jones, 'Womb of the Spirit', pp. 56–58; Spinks, 'Baptismal Patterns in Early Syria: Another Reading', p. 50.

[40] Johnson, *The Rites of Christian Initiation*, p. 80 (italics in original).

[41] Bryan D. Spinks, *Early and Medieval Rituals and Theologies of Baptism: From the New Testament to the Council of Trent* (Ashgate, Aldershot, 2006), p. 23.

[42] See *Didascalia* 5.9.1, 4; 6.12.2.

[43] *Didascalia* 2.33.1. The insertions in square brackets, suggested by Simon Jones ('Womb of the Spirit', p. 55), make sense of the second half of the sentence as being a reference to the bishops as those who gave new birth through the imposition of their hand in the immersion.

the pre-baptismal anointing because of the association of the anointing of the head with the unction of kings. In taking this view she had been preceded by a long line of scholars, many of them Anglicans eager to find an equivalent for the Western rite of confirmation here, even if that meant it preceded rather than followed the immersion.[44] But a passage in the *Didascalia* dealing with the reconciliation of penitents states:

> And just as you baptize a pagan and at that time receive him, so lay the hand upon this man while everyone is praying for him, and then bring him in and allow him to communicate with the church, for the imposition of the hand shall take the place of baptism for him, as whether by the imposition of a hand or by baptism they receive participation in the Holy Spirit.[45]

Simon Jones has argued that the word baptism here is meant to refer to the whole rite and not merely the act of immersion.[46] But surely if the compiler had envisaged the reception of the Spirit as emanating from the pre-baptismal imposition of hands with oil rather than the water, he would have noted the closeness of the parallel of the particular ritual action in the two cases? Although too much cannot be made of it, we may also note that in the sentence quoted above (*Didascalia* 2.33.2) the Spirit is mentioned after rather than before the gift of new birth. Nor is it necessary to conclude that just because the anointing is associated with kingly or priestly unction, it must also have been intended to denote the gift of the Spirit. In the North African tradition, the two are not so

---

[44] Among them, Gregory Dix, *The Theology of Confirmation in Relation to Baptism* (Dacre Press, London, 1946), p. 15; Ratcliff, 'The Old Syrian Baptismal Tradition', p. 26; G. G. Willis, 'What was the Earliest Syrian Baptismal Tradition?' in *Studia Evangelica* 6 (1973), p. 652. But it was also shared by Geoffrey Lampe, *The Seal of the Spirit* (Longmans, London, 1951), pp. 186–188, even though he rejected the sacramental nature of confirmation.

[45] *Didascalia* 2.41; English translation from Stewart-Sykes, *The Didascalia Apostolorum*, p. 162. See also *ibid.*, p. 74.

[46] Jones, 'Womb of the Spirit', p. 59.

intimately linked: initiation included both an anointing interpreted as the successor of the anointing of kings and priests and also a separate imposition of hands invoking the Holy Spirit.[47] Moreover, Chrysostom certainly understood the Spirit to be given in the water, as the passage quoted from one of his baptismal homilies earlier in this essay shows. While Winkler believed that this was the result of Chrysostom himself transferring it from an original association with the anointing of the head,[48] the presence of a similar understanding in the *Didascalia* points rather to a long-standing tradition of such an interpretation in those communities where the whole head and body were anointed before baptism, even if the Spirit was associated with the anointing in those communities that practised the anointing of the head alone.[49]

Initiation by anointing alone?

Because the sequence, anointing–baptism, cannot owe its origin to the model of the baptism of Jesus, what might account for it? In the case of the whole head and body anointing understood as providing protection and healing, its location before the immersion makes sense as a preparation for the central ritual. In the case of the anointing of the head alone, understood as transmission of the Holy Spirit, the order seems less logical. Sebastian Brock suggested that the conceptual model for this structure might have been the Jewish rite of initiation for male proselytes, circumcision followed by baptism, with the anointing understood as conferring the mark of new ownership as circumcision had done.[50] Another possibility, which does not exclude the first, has been raised by several scholars, and developed most fully by Susan Myers,[51]

---

[47] See Tertullian, *De baptismo* 7–8 (Whitaker, *Documents of the Baptismal Liturgy*, p. 9).

[48] Winkler, 'The Original Meaning of the Prebaptismal Anointing and its Implications', pp. 37–38.

[49] A similar claim, that the Spirit was understood to be conferred through the immersion in the *Didascalia*, was previously made by Whitaker, 'Unction in the Syrian Baptismal Rite'.

[50] Sebastian Brock, 'The Syrian Baptismal Rites' in *Concilium* 122 (1979), pp. 98–104, here at p. 99.

[51] Susan E. Myers, 'Initiation by Anointing in Early Syriac-Speaking Christianity' in *Studia Liturgica* 31 (2001), pp. 150–170; see also her *Spirit Epicleses in the Acts of Thomas* (Mohr Siebeck, Tübingen, 2010).

that baptism in water may not have been the universal rite of Christian initiation from the beginning, but that some communities might have practised initiation by anointing alone, a suggestion encouraged by the Greek version of *Acts of Judas* 49, which, contrary to the Syriac version, speaks only of 'sealing' and not baptism.[52] While such a proposal may seem odd in view of the later ubiquity of water baptism, it may not have appeared such a strange choice to the earliest Christian adherents. If Jesus was the Messiah, the Christ, i.e., 'the Anointed One', what could have been more natural than for his followers to be anointed on the head so that they too might be 'Christiani', anointed ones?

If there is any truth to this suggestion, then what we have in later practice would be a fusion of two rival traditions of initiation, anointing with oil and immersion in water, into one composite rite, as has often happened in the history of Christian liturgy when two variant texts or practices encounter one another. Rather than one being selected and the other abandoned, it has often proved expeditious to retain both, thereby both placating the supporters of each and ensuring that nothing that might be vital was eliminated from the liturgy.

The broader context

The only preliminaries to immersion mentioned in the *Didache* are teaching (presumably concerning the moral life that was outlined in the preceding Chapters 1—6) and fasting for one or two days. Nothing is said, for example, about a profession of faith. In the initiation stories in the *Acts of Thomas* preaching by the apostle leads the hearers to request baptism, but no other preliminaries are described. However, another passage in the *Didascalia* points to the existence of a more extended process, at least in some communities. The primary focus of this passage is on the action that should be taken against those Christians who have committed serious sins after they have been baptized, but it makes a comparison with the manner in which the unbaptized are treated:

---

[52] See the discussion in Kurt Niederwimmer, *The Didache: A Commentary*, Hermeneia series (Fortress, Minneapolis, 1998), pp. 165–167.

If he pays no attention he should be rebuked before the entire church, and if, moreover, he pays no attention to the entire church he should be accounted by you as a pagan or as a tax-collector. Because the Lord has said to you, bishops, that henceforth you should not receive anyone such into the church as a Christian, nor have any commerce with him, since you do not receive the pagan or the wicked tax-collector into the church, nor have anything to do with them, unless first they repent, and promise that they believe, and that thenceforth they shall do no evil deed....

Anyone who has been convicted of wicked deeds or of falsehood should be accounted by you as a pagan or as a tax-collector. Subsequently, should he promise to repent, like the pagans who promise and desire to repent, and who say 'I believe', and who are received into the assembly so that they may hear the word, but with whom we do not communicate until they have received the seal and become perfected, so we do not communicate with these until they show forth the fruits of repentance.[53]

This may look odd, in apparently expecting that converts would express their repentance and faith *before* they had been allowed to hear 'the word'. Clearly, there must have been some preliminary instruction designed to bring them to that point, very likely of an ethical kind such as we find in the *Didache*, but equally clearly, there was also a period of teaching of 'the word' after the profession of faith was made and before the initiation rites took place. Although we have no other explicit evidence for anything like this prior to the fourth century, comparative analysis suggests that it may well have been a common practice.

There is, first of all, a parallel pattern in the anonymous church order known as the *Apostolic Tradition of Hippolytus*. Here, after converts have undergone a first period of instruction, their moral conduct during

---

[53] *Didascalia* 2.38.3–4; 2.39.5–6; English translation from Stewart-Sykes, *The Didascalia Apostolorum*, pp. 160–161.

this time is examined: have they lived virtuously, have they honoured the widows, have they visited the sick, have they fulfilled every good work? Only when those sponsoring them testify that this is so, are they to be permitted to 'hear the gospel'.[54] While this public scrutiny of their changed behaviour replaces the personal profession of faith found in the *Didascalia*, a two-step catechumenate is common to both, with instruction in 'the word' or 'the gospel' being reserved to the final period of baptismal preparation for those who are judged sufficiently committed, whether by their own words or by the evidence of their life-style.

Neither source indicates how long this final stage might have lasted. The seventh-century West Syrian bishop and liturgical commentator James of Edessa claimed that after the candidates' renunciation and profession of faith 'the ancient custom was that they remained thus for a long time' before they were baptized,[55] but Maxwell Johnson's examination of later evidence from a variety of geographical regions has offered a more precise answer, pointing to the widespread existence of an apparently older three-week core embedded in the longer Lenten preparation for baptism of subsequent centuries.[56] Later evidence similarly suggests that the content of the first stage of instruction was primarily ethical and that of this second stage primarily doctrinal, out of which the Apostles' Creed emerged. While later Eastern rites continue to make the renunciation and profession of faith (*apotaxis/syntaxis*) the decisive turning point before baptism (even if no longer separated from it by such an extended period of time) with the recitation of the Trinitarian formula accompanying the immersion itself, the North African and Roman traditions instead continue to place the scrutinies in this position, with the profession of

---

[54] *Apostolic Tradition* 20.1. See Paul F. Bradshaw, Maxwell E. Johnson, and L. Edward Phillips, *The Apostolic Tradition: A Commentary* (Fortress Press, Minneapolis, 2002), p. 104.

[55] See Whitaker, *Documents of the Baptismal Liturgy*, p. 62.

[56] Maxwell E. Johnson, 'From Three Days to Forty Days: Baptismal Preparation and the Origins of Lent' in *Studia Liturgica* 20 (1990), pp. 185–201 = *idem* (ed.), *Living Water, Sealing Spirit*, pp. 118–136.

faith deferred until the moment of baptism itself, and only adopt the use of the Trinitarian formula at a much later date.[57]

Conclusion

If this study has been disappointingly inconclusive at a number of points, that is the nature of much study of early Christian liturgy. Because of the limited number and ambiguous character of many of the sources available to us, we must deal more often in probabilities than in certainties. And probabilities tend to involve a considerable measure of subjectivity. As we have seen earlier in this essay, the arguments put forward and the conclusions reached cannot always be divorced from the doctrinal presuppositions held by those engaging in the research, even if such biases are often quite unconscious. Short of the unlikely discovery of some entirely new source, the meaning of which would be transparent to all, we must often remain in the realm of the reinterpretation of existing material in the light of the most recent ways of thinking about how early Christianity developed. But because recent scholarship has moved away from the assumption of a highly centralized authority to one of more local autonomy and from trying to trace a single line of development in mainstream liturgical practice with only heretical offshoots deviating from this to the recognition of the essential pluriformity of worship patterns prior to the attempts at greater standardization in the course of the fourth century, it may fairly be claimed that the balance of probability lies with the conclusions reached in this essay.

---

[57] For a more detailed study of the evidence and of the process of change that took place, see Paul F. Bradshaw, *Reconstructing Early Christian Worship* (SPCK, London, 2009/Liturgical Press, Collegeville, 2010) chapters 4—5.

2

The Catechetical Lectures of Cyril of Jerusalem

A Source for the Baptismal Liturgy of Mid-Fourth Century Jerusalem[1]

Juliette Day

In *The Baptismal Liturgy of Jerusalem* I argued that the baptismal liturgy and theology contained in the *Mystagogical Catecheses* (*MC*) is quite different from that presented by Cyril of Jerusalem in the *Catechetical Lectures* (*Cats*) and that, consequently, it was not possible to attribute both works to the same author.[2] In order to sustain this conclusion, it is necessary to undertake a more detailed study of the baptismal liturgy presumed by Cyril in *Cats*, and to respond to the apparent challenge to my conclusions from Abraham Terian's subsequent study of the *Letter of Macarius to the Armenians*.[3] Furthermore, it is necessary to counter the tendency to conflate *Cats* and *MC* with the consequence that the liturgical outworking of the rich theology of *Cats* has been presumed to be found in *MC*, and conversely *MC* is used to provide rituals where these are lack-

---

[1] This paper, with minor modifications, was originally published in D. Hellholm, O. Norderval & C. Hellholm (eds), *Ablution, Initiation, and Baptism. Late Antiquity, Early Judaism and Early Christianity*, Beihefte zur Zeitschrift für die neutestamentliche Wissenschaft; vol. 176 (de Gruyter, Berlin, 2011), pp. 1179–1204.

[2] Juliette Day, *The Baptismal Liturgy of Jerusalem: 4th and 5th Century Evidence in Jerusalem, Egypt and Syria* (Ashgate, Aldershot, 2007).

[3] A. Terian, *Macarius of Jerusalem, Letter to the Armenians, A.D. 335* (St Vladimir's Seminary Press, New York, 2008).

ing in *Cats;* reliance on the *Letter of Macarius* as a relevant source simply exacerbates this. The ubiquity of such an approach can be demonstrated in much contemporary scholarship: in general surveys of early baptismal practice (e.g. Lampe; Johnson);[4] in editions and monographs of Cyril of Jerusalem's lectures (e.g. Yarnold; Doval);[5] and more recently, in Everett Ferguson's magisterial study *Baptism in the Early Church.*[6]

The primary purpose here will be to establish what baptismal liturgy concluded the catecheses delivered by Cyril in 351.[7] Because an explicit discussion of the baptismal liturgy was not Cyril's aim in *Cats*, we shall have carefully to discern where he might be referring to actual liturgical practice, where he might be implying such a practice, and where biblical and theological motifs might be mistaken for liturgical practice. Determining the value of Cyril's words as liturgical evidence will depend upon the context in which they occur in *Cats* and their conformity to his theological narrative of baptism. As we shall see, the liturgical evidence in *Cats* has to be gleaned from various locations and then organized according to the ritual structure which *Cats* itself indicates; in turn, the proposed structure itself must be tested in light of the conclusions about the content, purpose and position of each liturgical unit.

One hypothesis arising from my study of *MC* was that it appeared to demonstrate influence by a tradition similar to that of the family of the *Apostolic Tradition* (*AT*). Testing this hypothesis also requires a more precise establishment of the baptismal liturgy and theology of *Cats* in order that the distinctiveness of *MC* can be fully demonstrated; this study will conclude with some reflections upon the relationship between the Jerusalem sources and the versions of *AT*.

---

[4] G. W. H. Lampe, *The Seal of the Spirit: A Study in the Doctrine of Baptism and Confirmation in the New Testament and the Fathers* (Longmans, London, 1951); Maxwell E. Johnson, *The Rites of Christian Initiation* (The Liturgical Press, Collegeville, 1999).

[5] E. J. Yarnold, 'The Authorship of the Mystagogical Catecheses attributed to Cyril of Jerusalem' in *Heythrop Journal*, 19 (1978), pp. 143–161; A. Doval, *Cyril of Jerusalem, Mystagogue: The Authorship of the Mystagogic Catecheses* (CUA Press, Washington, 2001).

[6] E. Ferguson, *Baptism in the Early Church: History, Theology and Liturgy in the First Five Centuries* (Eerdmans, Grand Rapids, 2009), pp. 473–487.

[7] For the date of *Cats*, see A. Doval, 'The Date of Cyril of Jerusalem's Catecheses' in *Journal of Theological Studies* 48 (1997), pp. 129–132.

Cats and the *Letter of Macarius of Jerusalem to the Armenians* (*Ep.Mac.*)

In a review in *Worship*, Maxwell Johnson suggested that my conclusions regarding the authorship of *MC* might well be challenged by Abraham Terian's new edition of the *Letter to the Armenians* by Macarius of Jerusalem.[8] Terian's aim was twofold: to produce a new English translation of the text, and to assert that the *Letter* is to be rightly attributed to Macarius, predecessor to Cyril in the see of Jerusalem and that it can be dated to 335. *Ep.Mac.* is pertinent to our project here, because the information it provides concerning the baptismal liturgy appears to indicate that a rite like that of *MC* 1—3 was in use in Jerusalem at a date much earlier than even those asserting Cyrilline authorship would propose. A methodological consequence of this is, therefore, that it is right and proper to conflate the liturgical information of *Cats* and *MC*, and of course now *Ep.Mac.*, which indeed Terian attempts.[9]

This letter, retained in two Armenian sources, is a response from Macarius, bishop of Jerusalem (314—335/6), to questions about church discipline and the administration of the sacraments put to him by a delegation of Armenian priests who have witnessed the rites in Jerusalem and have found their own practices to be negligent. The sections on baptism are very short and are preserved in three quite different redactions: the first is a more complete version in the *Book of Letters*, compiled in the early seventh century with a subsequent arrangement in 1298; the second, in the *Liber Canonum* compiled in the early eighth century and completed in the fourteenth.[10] The third is in the form of a lengthy quotation in a discourse on Epiphany by Anania of Shirak (c. 690), and the same extract appears in a discourse

---

[8] M. E. Johnson, Review of *The Baptismal Liturgy of Jerusalem* in *Worship* 82.1 (2008), pp. 89–91. He has repeated this more recently in 'Baptismal Liturgy in fourth-century Jerusalem in the Light of Recent Scholarship' in Basilius J. Groen, Steven Hawkes Teeples and Stefanos Alexopoulos (eds), *Inquiries into Eastern Christian Worship: Selected Papers of the Second International Congress of the Society of Oriental Liturgy*, Rome, 17–21 September 2008, *Eastern Christian Studies*, Vol. 12 (Peeters, Leuven, 2012), pp. 81–98.

[9] See Terian, p. 112 for one such example of the conflation of sources.

on the Nativity by Anania of Sanahin (c. 1070); the latter is based on that of the earlier Anania and so this forms only one witness.[11]

In the *Liber Canonum*, the 'various injunctions contained in the Letter were enumerated in the form of ecclesiastical canons', and thus the epistolary form is not so evident; however, the *Letter's* lengthy prologue was preserved, which led Terian to conclude that not much had been lost in the process.[12] We will note, though, that the sections on baptism differ greatly in the sources and this alerts us to need to pay attention to genre in evaluating liturgical evidence. We would not expect a collection of canons to preserve intact regulations which no longer apply; thus, we see that the injunctions to baptize at Epiphany, Easter and Pentecost in the Anania fragment are absent from the *Liber Canonum*, because, at the time of compilation, baptism was no longer performed at fixed points during the year.[13] Again, in *Ep.Mac.* 221,7—12, the *Liber Canonum* has Macarius forbid deacons to baptize, 'this authority belongs to bishops and priests alone, and that it is not right for deacons to perform it, for they are attendants...'[14] We will see below (4c) that this is contradicted by Cyril who indicates that deacons do baptize; clearly, then, a redactor has been at work.[15] *Ep.Mac.* also furnishes us with indications of the structure of the rite: a renunciation of Satan (220, 12); triple immersion in imitation of Christ's death and resurrection (223, 4); imposition of hands 'with right confession of faith' for the bestowal of the Holy Spirit (223, 9) by bishops

---

[10] *Ibid.*, p. 18.

[11] *Ibid.*, p. 63.

[12] *Ibid.*, p. 19.

[13] Contrast the fragment in Anania of Shirak 284(5) where it states, 'Hence the ordinance of baptism of the holy font and the earnest observance of the three feasts during which those who are dedicated to God desire most eagerly to bring unto baptism ... which is carried out on these holy and prominent days'; with *Liber Canonum* 223, 1–3, 'Nor is the administration (of the rite) on major feasts only, for the Apostles were baptizing with a preference for the feasts, but, to the satisfaction of those who came to them, were illuminating by making rebirth through the waters possible.' (*Ibid.*, p. 83).

[14] *Ibid.*, p. 81.

[15] Terian believes that the 'views of the two bishops are not irreconcilable', even though he precedes this by noting that 'some redaction may be suspected' (p. 115).

and priests only (225, 9—10); anointing with the 'oil of holiness' (223, 11) blessed preferably by the 'chief-bishop' for use by other bishops (225, 11).

Again and again, Terian acknowledges that the liturgical information has been subject to later redaction, but he does not take that into account when asserting the value of this text as evidence of the liturgical practice of Jerusalem in the mid-fourth century, and especially when conflating the evidence of *Ep.Mac.*, *Cats* and *MC* to produce a composite rite as he does on page 112. Thus, he says, 'Some deletions resulting from changes in later practice, as also from theologically motivated tampering, are detectable ...' (p. 23); 'there is a substantive tampering in the baptismal part of the text.... Moreover there is glaring evidence for repeated post-Chalcedonian tampering in the eucharistic part ...' (p. 43); 'The excerpt (from Anania of Shirak) clearly reveals that the text of the Letter in the *Kanonagirk* has undergone some changes, ranging from abridgement to alteration...' (p. 68); in relation to the eucharistic sections the text is 'maligned' (p. 71). He notes that the Letter was rejected by the compilers of the original epistolary of the Armenian Church because 'certain of its recommendations ... conflicted with the rite of baptism in vogue at the time when the compilation was put together', and that 'for the same reasons the document was left out of the various compilations of the *Kanonagirk* until it was modified for inclusion in the eleventh-century edition' (p. 73). Terian's own words alert us most clearly to the need for extreme caution when using the liturgical evidence of the *Letter*; this is not to deny that Macarius did indeed write a letter to the Armenian Church in 335, but simply to warn that our version does not seem to be the original.

What use can we make then of the letter? The following analysis of the baptismal liturgy which can be inferred from *Cats* will demonstrate that the Jerusalem rite has undergone a substantial structural change by the time of the composition of *MC* 1—3. Were we able to find *Ep.Mac.* to be a reliable witness to the rite of 335, then we would be in the envious position of being able to determine precisely which elements of the rite Cyril himself inherited and which he had modified. *Ep.Mac.* attests to the presence of some elements which are constant features of the Jerusalem rite and which, in any case, are commonplace in fourth century baptismal liturgies (the renunciation of Satan, a triple immersion); but it also presents us with some liturgical units which are doubtful in *Cats* and absent from *MC* (the imposition of hands), and it is vague about the position and type of the anointing with the 'oil of holiness', which Terian suggests has been subject to redaction in light of *MC*.[16] We share Terian's hesitations about assigning the liturgical information to the time of Macarius, but unlike him we are not prepared to use this information to produce a composite rite for Jerusalem based additionally upon a conflation of *Cats* and *MC*. The liturgical sections of *Ep. Mac.* should be considered the fruit of several layers of redaction, such that assigning them to a particular date or even to Jerusalem itself with any degree of accuracy is impossible.

The Jordan Event as the Biblical–Theological Narrative of Baptism in *Cats*

In catechetical and homiletical works one finds that authors tend to interpret baptism in light of one dominant typology, even though they are likely to refer to many other relevant, and sometimes even more obscure, passages of scripture. The choice of dominant typology indicates the author's understanding of how the benefits of baptism are conveyed to the candidate by the rite itself and, thus, typological preference will be determined by the ritual sequence and content, or indeed, conversely, a new typological awareness might cause a revision of a rite.[17] The investigation of biblical typology is key to identifying the evolution of the baptismal liturgy in Jerusalem. Elsewhere, I have discussed how *MC* uses Romans 6 for the immersion but as that provides no theology for the post-immersion chrismation, the author turns to the Jordan event;[18] in *Cats*, however, Cyril's preferred typology is the Jordan event, with

---

[16] *Ibid.*, p. 126.

[17] Proposed by G. Winkler in relation to the adoption of Romans 6 typology in 'The Original Meaning of the Prebaptismal Anointing and its Implications', *Worship* 52 (1978), pp. 24–45.

scant reference to Romans 6 despite a very extensive presentation of scriptural warrants for baptism throughout *Cats*. In what follows, we will show how Cyril's use of the Jordan event, predominantly taken from Matthew, reveals his distinctive theological method.

Cyril's theology is thoroughly biblical, and the modern reader cannot help but be amazed, not just at the extent of his knowledge of scripture, but also the way in which he places quite diverse scriptural texts in juxtaposition to explain key theological points. In an article on Cyril's Pneumatology, I showed how he selects and arranges biblical quotations to form a theological argument without any supplementary comment or explanation; these passages are not proof texts rather they construct the theological discourse itself.[19] In *Cat*. 3, though, he adopts a different method in which he isolates the different events within the narrative of Christ's baptism and using them sequentially as the starting point for an exploration of different theological aspects of baptism. So the Jordan event is not used typologically to explain the liturgy of baptism and its effect upon the candidates, but rather provides a structural template for Cyril's discourse. Thus the lecture opens with John's exhortation to 'Make ready the way of the Lord', and continues through John's preaching of baptism for the repentance of sins, to the baptism of Christ, the beginning of his ministry with the forty days in the desert and the beginning of preaching. Each part of the narrative of Christ's baptism is used by Cyril to commence an explanation of a key theme in the theology of baptism and salvation and the effects upon the candidates. In places the theological point extrapolated is quite tangential to the narrative element which precedes it, sometimes relying only on a single common word.

The narrative of the Jordan event begins in the opening words of the lecture with, 'a voice of one crying in the desert: Prepare the way of the Lord' (3.1 and 3.2) applied to John; Cyril takes up the theme of preparation

---

[18] See my *The Baptismal Liturgy of Jerusalem*, pp. 6–8; 65–68.

[19] 'Cyril of Jerusalem on the Holy Spirit' in V. Twomey and J. E. Rutherford (eds), *The Holy Spirit in the Fathers of the Church: Proceedings of the Seventh Irish Patristics Symposium* (Four Courts Press, Dublin, 2010).

and discourses upon preparedness for the (mystical) marriage feast. The candidates are to 'begin to wash your garments by repentance' so to be clean on entering the bridal chamber; the bridegroom invites all but will reject those who did not enter with 'a wedding garment' (Matt. 22.12); those permitted to enter might say 'Let my soul rejoice in the Lord: for he has clothed me with a garment of salvation and a robe of gladness; like a bridegroom he placed a diadem on me, like a bride he has adorned me with ornaments' (Isa. 61.10 LXX).

There follows a discursive section on the baptismal water and its effects (discussed below in relation to the immersion) with little biblical imagery and quotation. This is followed by a list of Old Testament events in which water played a part in effecting salvation or transformation (the parting of the Red Sea, the Flood, the priesting of Aaron: *Cat.* 3.5). He returns to the Jordan event with the comment that 'Baptism is the end of the Old Testament and the beginning of the New' and that John was the last of the prophets (3.6). That this is so, he demonstrates by quoting the opening of Mark's Gospel, "The beginning of the gospel of Jesus Christ", and following, "There came John baptizing in the desert". From this part of the narrative, Cyril discourses on John's greatness compared to the other prophets (by way of Elijah, Enoch and Moses) and of his worthiness to fulfil that role:

> Do you see what a great man God chose to be the initiator of this grace? He was living in poverty and loving solitude, but not hating people; he ate locusts and put wings to his soul; he was satisfied with honey and spoke sweeter and yet more satisfying [words]; he wore a garment of camel's hair and displayed in himself a model of asceticism; who, while yet carried in his mother's womb, was sanctified by the Holy Spirit ... For since the grace of baptism is so great, great too must be its patron. (*PG* 33:436)

Despite being based upon the biblical narrative, there is little in this section which develops Cyril's theology of baptism, although he does promote John as a model of the ascetic life.

Cyril connects the narrative with his audience by reminding them that all Jerusalem went out to John at the Jordan because 'the honour of all good things belongs to Jerusalem'(3.7; *PG* 33:436–7). But it is not sufficient merely to go to the Jordan [i.e. the font], they must go 'confessing their sins', so that John may apply the remedy to the wounds (sin) which they display. Cyril quotes John's words to the people as warnings to the catechumens. First, in Matthew 3.7, 'Brood of vipers, who told you to flee from the wrath to come?', which Cyril interprets as salvation from the eternal fire for those who believe and are baptized *with John's baptism*. And secondly, a warning against hypocritical pretence of piety, or against an attitude like that of Simon Magus, is accompanied with John's prophecy that the axe has been laid to the root and that not judged good will be burned in the fire (Matt. 3.10). To avoid the charge of hypocrisy the catechumens are reminded of their responsibility for the poor, 'You wish to enjoy the grace of the Holy Spirit, but can you not find the poor worthy of physical food?' (3.8; *PG* 33:438); and that they will receive forgiveness of their past sins whatever they might have been.

Returning to the narrative in Matthew's Gospel, where John announces that one is to come who will baptize with water and fire (Matt. 3.11), Cyril presents the difference between John's baptism and that of Christ (3.9). The Son of God is greater than John, he says, as the Word of God is greater than the herald, and the one who baptizes with water is surpassed by the one who baptizes with the Holy Spirit and fire; Cyril illustrates this with the descent of the Holy Spirit as fire upon the apostles at Pentecost (Acts 2.2–4). But, curiously, Cyril concludes this section with the validity of martyrs' baptism in their own blood in time of persecution and the importance of the confession of faith.

Having already shown that John's baptism does not confer the same benefits as baptism in Christ, and having emphasized that Christ is greater than John, he needs now to explain why Christ submitted to baptism by John. Cyril states that baptism is sanctified because Jesus himself submitted to it, and thus it should not be considered unnecessary (3.11). Christ was not baptized for the remission of sins, but that 'divine grace and dignity might be given to those who are baptized' (*PG* 33:441). Again Cyril departs from the narrative to discuss Christ's destruction of the dragon who inhabits the water (cf. Job) and, consequently, those who are baptized are saved from death. It is here that Cyril makes his only reference to the lection appended at the head of *Cat.* 3, Romans 6:

> You descend dead in sin, you come up made alive in righteousness; for if you have been planted together in the likeness of the Saviour's death, you shall be deemed worthy too of his resurrection. For just as Jesus died carrying the sins of the whole world so that by putting sin to death he might rise in righteousness so, too, do you descend into the water, buried in the water as he was in the rock, and you rise up again 'walking in the newness of life'. (*Cat.* 3.12; *PG* 33:444)

The narrative continues with Christ's sojourn in the wilderness: as Christ fought against demons for 40 days after baptism, so the candidates will be strengthened to do battle and preach the gospel after baptism (3.13). The correct order of things was established by Christ who did not preach until 'the Holy Spirit had descended upon him in the bodily form of a dove' (3.14 [Luke 3.22]; *PG* 33:444). The purpose of the descent of the Spirit upon Jesus was so that John could recognize him according to the prophecy he had received, for obviously Christ 'knew him even before he came in bodily form'. So, too, upon the candidates the Holy Spirit comes down upon you, and a fatherly voice comes over you: not, 'This is my Son', but, 'This has now become my son'. For upon that one 'is', ... since he is always 'Son of God'; but upon you 'has now become', since you do not have it by nature, but receive sonship by adoption. (*PG* 33:445)

At no point in *Cats* does Cyril tell the candidates the story of the Jordan event, and he must have presumed that it was familiar to the candidates. This raises doubts about the veracity of the Romans 6 lection at the head of *Cat.* 3; it is listed as the lection for the third Lenten catechesis in the *Armenian Lectionary*, which is contemporary with *MC* and where Romans 6 would be appropriate in light of the typology of that rite. Indeed, Romans

6 is rarely cited or alluded to by Cyril; apart from 3.12 (above) he makes no connection between Christ's death and resurrection and baptism, not even in *Cat.* 13 on the Passion, nor in *Cat.* 14 on the resurrection. Cyril uses the Jordan event to provide a structure for his theological explanation of baptism, but does so in ways which are far from straightforward. *Cat.* 3 is punctuated with quotations and paraphrases from the gospel accounts of the event, but he does not expound these; rather, he uses them to present additional, and sometime tangential, themes. And we note that he does not apply the narrative typologically to the rite of baptism; there are some references to the liturgy itself in this lecture but that is not his purpose; however, no other biblical passage receives quite such prominence in *Cats* indicating that it was key to his understanding of the rite and its theology.

The Liturgy of Baptism in *Cats*

Using *Cats* to determine the liturgy of baptism is complicated by Cyril's purpose being quite other than a systematic account of the rite; the main purpose of the lectures is an explanation of the creed (*Cats* 5—18) with four introductory lectures (an introduction/exhortation, on faith, on baptism and on repentance). Not even in the lecture on baptism (*Cat.* 3) does Cyril provide us with a description of the rite; as we have just seen, this lecture delivers a theology of baptism based upon the account of the Jordan event. So what sort of material might reveal the liturgy? The evidence is both positive and negative. First, Cyril gives us direct and indirect allusions to rituals, which need to be assessed for the 'balance of probability' that they refer to liturgical actions. The 'negative evidence' may in places be more convincing, although it is an unusual way of proceeding. Our investigation into the baptismal rite of mid-fourth-century Jerusalem occurs in the context of the ritual pattern and content of other fourth-century rites, most notably the liturgy of *MC* 1—3. Thus we are justified in asking whether some of the rituals common to these are hinted at in *Cats*, or, conversely, does Cyril by his words *exclude* the presence of certain rituals. Additionally, given the 'more satisfying' evidence of *MC* and the presumption of an evolution of the rite, where theology or typology is in direct contrast to that of *MC*, we may presume that *Cats* presents us with an earlier liturgical form.

In what follows we have gathered the key evidence for the sequence of the rite, the ministers and then each liturgical unit drawn from *Cats* alone. Where other Jerusalem or Palestinian sources provide corroboration of the conclusions drawn, or indeed furnish us with 'negative evidence', they will be discussed. No attempt will be made here to infer the manner or evolution from the liturgy of *Cats* to that of *MC* which will take place in the concluding section.

The Sequence of the Rite

Establishing the ritual sequence of the rite will provide a structure upon which to hang the disparate evidence, and which can be tested in our investigation of each liturgical unit. In three places Cyril provides some ambiguous information, none more so than the first of these. In *Cat.* 1.2, it is possible that he is alluding to the rituals and their benefits:

> By confession, put off the old man which is being corrupted through his deceptive lusts, so that you might put on the new ... . By faith take hold of the pledge of the Holy Spirit ... Come forward for the mystical seal ... Be counted among the holy and spiritual flock of Christ ... . (*PG* 33:372)

It is possible that Cyril here refers to each stage of the rite: that is the confession of sin, the profession of faith, sealing (by the immersion) and the eucharist.

Clearer indications of the sequence appear in what are two separate notices of further instruction at the end of the final lecture. How one interprets the juxtaposition of two such notices which do not agree in detail is dependent upon the relationship between *Cats* and *MC*. If indeed *MC* was preached after *Cats*, and the liturgy of the former concludes the latter, then it is perfectly justifiable to apportion the references in *Cat.* 18.32 and 18.33 to the known liturgical sequence of *MC* 1—3; such was the conclusion of Gifford, Yarnold and Doval. If, however, one concludes that *MC* is not related to the liturgy presumed in *Cats*, then alternative explanations are required. Thus one could propose that the two notices refer to different instructions, or that the second of these, which is close in structure to *MC* 1—3, is an interpolation made with the express purpose of harmonizing the two series of lectures. My earlier work on *MC* and the discussion of the baptismal liturgy of *Cats* which follows discounts the conclusions of Gifford, Yarnold and Doval; and we are not minded to assume that 18.33 is an interpolation, given that it is contained in all manuscripts, thus we assume that at the end of *Cat.* 18 Cyril provides notice of two distinct instructions.

The first, in 18.32, appears to be notice of something like a rehearsal at which the candidates would learn what they are to do in the liturgy:

> The rest is appointed for the holy day of Easter when your love of Christ is enlightened by the washing of regeneration, you will be again instructed about what is necessary, God willing: with what piety and order you ought to go in when called; the purpose of each of the holy mysteries of baptism and with what reverence and order you ought to go from the baptism to the holy altar of God there to enjoy its spiritual and heavenly mysteries. (*PG* 33:1053)

Thus, on the morning of Holy Saturday (they will be baptized that evening) they will be told how to behave, what the different rituals are and then about the eucharist. We learn from this that the candidates will be 'called in', either individually or as a group they will be invited into the baptistery; there is more than one 'mystery' of baptism, and finally they receive the eucharist.

The second notice is clearly to tell them to attend the mystagogical instruction in the week following Easter, beginning on the Monday:

> In these you will be given the reasons for each thing which has happened ...; first concerning that happening before baptism; next how you were cleansed of your sins by the Lord, by the washing of water with the word; and how like priests you have become sharers

in the name of Christ and how the seal of the fellowship of the Holy
Spirit was given to you; and about the mysteries at the altar of the
new covenant ... how you ought to approach them and when and
how to receive them; ... . (18.33; *PG* 33:1056)

How we allocate the topics in this syllabus to different liturgical units
depends on how we interpret the scant evidence in *Cats*. Clearly there
are rituals before baptism, the number and type of these pre-immersion
rituals is not specified, and there is a clear reference to the immersion. But
do the catechumens become 'sharers in the name' and receive the 'seal of
the fellowship of the Holy Spirit' as a consequence of the immersion, or in
two separate post-immersion rituals, or even by a single post-immersion
ritual? As we can see the relationship of 'seal' to an anointing and the
presence of other post-immersion rituals such as an imposition of hands
or signing with the cross will be key in interpreting this section.

If we extrapolate the information from these three passages and present
it in tabular form, we can see how this evidence alone does not provide a
coherent ritual sequence, and where they diverge from each other further
investigation of Cyril's other references to each individual liturgical unit will
be required.

Cat. 1	*Cat.* 18.32	*Cat.* 18.33
	Summons to baptistery	
Confession of sin	Multiple baptismal rituals	Pre-immersion ritual(s)
Profession of faith		
Sealing		Immersion
		'Sharers in the name'
		Sealing
Eucharist	Eucharist	Eucharist

Putting all these together, we arrive at the following structure for the
rite:

- summons to baptistery,
- confession of sin,
- profession of faith,
- EITHER immersion which also denotes 'partaking of the name' and 'sealing',
- OR immersion followed by one or two post-immersion rituals,
- eucharist.

In the discussion which follows we will assess the evidence for the pre-immersion rituals of confession (renunciation) and profession (adherence), and for the manner of conducting the immersion. The meaning of 'seal' in *Cats* is crucial to determining the presence, number and type of any post-immersion rituals, and we will hunt for evidence of an anointing, or imposition of hands, or ritual consignation.

The Ministers of the Rite

In presenting the conclusions to my discussion of the baptismal liturgy of *MC*, I made some suggestions about the number and type of ministers which that liturgy seemed to require. The role of the bishop was ambiguous: he may have conducted one or more liturgical units within the baptistery, or may only have been present. But, in addition, we suggested that a number of deacons would be required for the pre-immersion rituals and perhaps also a presbyter, if the bishop had a passive role. *Ep.Mac.*, as we have noted already, regulates who may be the ministers of baptism, expressly forbidding deacons who 'are attendants; consequently it (baptism) is closed to them' (221, 11).[20] Were we to accept that *Ep.Mac.* contains accurate liturgical information from 335, it would indeed be strange to find that Cyril had apparently reversed what Macarius presents as 'an ordinance of the church'. Cyril himself is much more ambiguous on the rank of the baptizing minister:

---

[20] Terian, p. 81.

> For at the time of baptism, when you approach the bishops, or priests or deacons (for the grace is everywhere, in the countryside and in the towns; ...) approach then the minister of baptism; not approaching the face of the one you see before you, but remember the Holy Spirit ... . (*Cat.* 17.35; *PG* 33:1009)

For Cyril, it is the faith of the candidate which is truly effective: '... if you approach with faith, men will minister to you visibly, but the Holy Spirit will give you what is not visible' (17.36; *PG* 33:1009). If the ban on diaconal baptism was truly in force, Cyril would have been unlikely to include deacons in his list of baptizing ministers; however, nowhere does he use the first person and so we cannot be sure what ritual(s) were reserved to the bishop.

The Pre-Immersion Rituals

In my earlier writing on *MC*, I remarked that the evidence from that text alone seemed to imply that the baptismal liturgy of Jerusalem had undergone a revision, but that newly introduced liturgical units had not yet been fully integrated. This is especially the case with the pre-immersion rituals. From the conclusion of *The Baptismal Liturgy of Jerusalem*:

> We have noted how the renunciation and adherence sequence in *MC* seems to function as a self-contained unit; this seems apparent from the instructions about orientation which do not fit the topography of the Holy Sepulchre complex and by what seems to be the 'ritual incoherence' of the candidates receiving exorcized oil after having declared their allegiance. There is, additionally, a duplication of the confessions of faith: the first, a natural counterpart to the renunciation in both content and rhythm; the second elicited by the interrogation accompanying the immersions. These factors seem to hint at a possible re-organization of the pre-immersion rituals; we do not necessarily wish to conclude that they are an addition to the rite,

but merely suggest that the form in which they are presented may be new.[21]

If this is correct then *MC* might provide some 'negative' evidence of what the preliminary rituals of the earlier rite might have been.

The Renunciation

If it is the case that the Jerusalem rite underwent a change in the type, number and meaning of the renunciatory rituals, is there evidence of a presumed earlier pattern in *Cats*? The 'ritual incoherence' of *MC* is caused by the presence of an exorcistic anointing to 'drive out all trace of the enemy' (*MC* 2.3; *PG* 33:1080) occurring after a declaration of adherence, which itself follows a statement of renunciation. This would seem to indicate that, even after having declared his allegiance, the candidate had not fully dealt with the influence of Satan and sin, and that these needed to be purged before entering the font. In *MC*, the renunciation is made by the candidate facing West, who repeated each clause after a minister: 'I renounce you Satan', 'and all your works', 'and all your pomp', 'and all your service'. An anointing with exorcized oil occurred after the profession of faith.

In *Cats*, Cyril does not refer to a liturgical and formulaic renunciation of Satan, but does continually exhort them to repentance. It is possible that the candidates did, though, make a formal confession of sins at some point, because in *Cat.* 1.5 they are exhorted to confess now, 'at the accepted time' and on the day of salvation (*Cat.* 1.5; *PG* 33:376). By 'accepted time', might he not refer to a specific occasion on which this took place, that is at their baptism? The context of this statement is a section which refers to other parts of the process, the exorcisms and the catecheses, and so it would not be over-speculative to assume he does mean a liturgical act in which they confessed their sins. We would not expect the liturgical fulfilment of a confession to be the renunciatory formula and ritual described in *MC* 1; however, we might suggest that an exorcistic ritual may serve as an effective

---

[21] *The Baptismal Liturgy of Jerusalem*, p. 133.

conclusion to a full and sincere confession leading to the blotting out of sin in the waters of baptism.[22] This may not necessarily have been conducted using oil, as there is no reference to oil in *Cats*, but the exorcistic anointing in *MC* may preserve in a new form an earlier exorcistic ritual, which followed a confession of sin.

The Adherence

Our analysis of the renunciation ritual in *MC* applies also to the adherence: we have suggested that the eastward-facing statement of belief (adherence) duplicates the second affirmation of faith made in response to the interrogation in the font, and we have rejected the orientation of the adherence as being an original feature. That there was a confession of faith seems certain from *Cat.* 3.10 when, in the context of a discussion of the martyrs' baptism by blood, he says,

> The martyrs also confess (their faith), 'becoming a show for the world, for angels and men'; and you too will confess in a short while; but now is not the time for you to hear about these things. (*Cat.* 3.10; *PG* 33:440–1)

The martyrs make their confession at their baptism, that is a baptism in blood, and, by inference, the candidates will make a confession at their baptism, this time in water. This is not the only time when Cyril says that he will explain something later on; it also occurs in reference to a supplementary rite for the bestowal of the Holy Spirit. The question for us, is what value to we attach to such statements given that the promised explanation of either does not occur in *Cats*?

We can exclude the recitation of the creed as a ritual of adherence within the baptismal liturgy. The creed is delivered to the candidates at the end of *Cat.* 5, after a summary of the ten main points of doctrine. The

---

[22] See *Cat.* 15.23 (*PG* 33: 901–4): 'Your every act of covetousness is written; your every act of lust is written; every false oath, blasphemy, sorcery, theft and murder is written. All these things are recorded if you do them after having been baptized; for what went before has been deleted.'

creed is presented as the topic of the whole catechesis and as a standard of faith to last after their baptism: Cyril urges them, 'Keep this as a resource throughout the whole course of your life, ...' (5.12; *PG* 33:520). That the creed is not part of any confession of faith in the baptismal rite is indicated by the communal recitation which Cyril leads in the middle of the final lecture. The candidates are not tested on this individually but Cyril says, 'Again, I shall say the profession of faith for you, recite these words by yourself with all care and memorize them' (18.21; *PG* 33: 1041). Egeria's description of a final scrutiny at which the creed was recited by each candidate before the bishop would not appear to be correct for the mid-fourth century.[23]

Sealing

The use by Cyril in *Cats* of 'seal' to describe what happens in baptism and its complete absence from *MC* 1—3[24] is significant in demonstrating the different treatment of initiation in these two sources and strengthens the case for assigning these texts to different authors. It is difficult to accept that in 351 Cyril would have considered the 'seal of the Holy Spirit' to be a key aspect of baptism, but (if one accepts the conclusions of Yarnold and Doval about the date of *MC*), after returning from the Council of Constantinople, he would have re-organized his rite to provide an explicit ritual for the gift of the Spirit (the post-immersion anointing with chrism), with no reference to 'sealing'. The absence of *sphragis* in *MC* seems to us to be a significant criterion for attributing that work to anyone other than Cyril.

Although 'seal' can be applied to an effect of the baptismal rite or of a particular ritual, it may also be applied to a specific ritual which conveys the attribute received, most commonly to an anointing or a

---

[23] *It.Eg.* 46.5:'... the bishop comes early to the Great Church, the Martyrium. His chair is placed at the back of the apse, behind the altar, and one by one the candidates go up to the bishop, men with their fathers and women with their mothers, and repeat the Creed to him.' (J. Wilkinson, *Egeria's Travels*, 3rd edn, Ayris and Phillips, Warminster, 1999, p. 163).

[24] In *MC* 4.7–8, 'seal' is used only once in a citation from Psalm 25.

hand-laying. In our investigation of seal in *Cats* we note that Cyril most commonly applies it to the immersion, but there are a variety of other uses, none of them original to Cyril, which do not presume a particular ritual. In *Cat.* 1.5, the seal is given to those who 'come forward', that is, present themselves for baptism, and who demonstrate a worthy motive, presumably by repenting of their sins and declaring their faith. It is a mark of ownership in 1.2 and 1.3: in the former related to the brand on sheep; in the latter to the brand on soldiers. The seal is not necessarily visible to the eye or to other people, but it is recognized by the Lord, by angels and by demons. The seal is never described in purely physical terms by Cyril: it is, for example, the 'holy indissoluble seal' (*Procat.* 16; *PG* 33:360); 'indelible' (*Procat.* 17; *PG* 33:365); 'mystical' (1.2; *PG* 33:372); 'spiritual and saving' (1.3; *PG* 33:373). We also find him using the term with the sense of safeguarding, a locking away, or preserving in *Cat.* 1.5, where the candidates are to 'seal by faith' that which they have heard in the catecheses. A further indication that the seal is not physical occurs in *Cat.* 3.3:

> Each one of you is about to stand before God, before the myriad ranks of angels; the Holy Spirit is about to seal your souls; you are to be enrolled in the army of the great King. (*PG* 33:428)

The sealing occurs before the 'angels', that is in heaven, it does not occur in front of the ministers. And, of course, the purpose of the seal is not a physical marking, its effects are spiritual and are known only in the spiritual realm – it is recognized by angels and by demons, and is the sign by which God recognizes his own. In the human and worldly realm, it is possible for the baptized to conceal that they have been sealed through sin, heresy and unbelief; however, none of this removes the seal, which is in any case 'indelible' (*Procat.* 17).

Even if the seal itself is not physical, it is, though, given (by God, not the minister) by, with and through the water: sealing is co-terminous with the ritual act, but is not effected by it. Cyril makes this clear in numerous places of which this passage is key:

> Each one of you is about to stand before God, before the myriad ranks of angels; the Holy Spirit is about to seal your souls; you are to be enrolled in the army of the great King. Prepare yourselves, therefore; make yourselves ready; not by putting on shining garments, but piety of soul and a good conscience. Do not consider the water to be for a ordinary washing, but consider the spiritual grace being given with the water. ... For since man is twofold, composed of soul and body, the cleansing is also twofold, incorporeal for the incoporeal part, bodily for the bodily. When the water washes the body, the Spirit seals the soul; so that having our heart sprinkled by the Spirit and our body washed in clean water, we may approach God. (*Cat.* 3.3–4; *PG* 33:428–9)

That Cyril is indeed speaking about seal in relation to the water specifically, and not using 'baptism' as shorthand for the whole rite of initiation, is clear from the discussion which follows of the appropriateness of the element of water to convey spiritual benefits, demonstrated by references to the Old Testament (3.5). He refers to the Spirit hovering over the waters at creation; the crossing of the Red Sea as liberation and hence 'freedom for the world from sin comes through the washing by water in the Word of God'; from the Flood, he reasons, 'wherever there is a covenant, there is water'; and priesthood is conveyed after washing, following the example of Aaron, 'Aaron first washed and then became high priest'. The descent of the Spirit at the moment of immersion is guaranteed by the example of Jesus' own baptism:

> If you have sincere piety, the Holy Spirit will descend upon you too, and the voice of the Father above will be heard over you; not 'This is my Son', but 'This has now become my son'. (3.14; *PG* 33:444–5)

The second principal use of 'seal' is, though, a physical and ritual action, but not one associated with the initiation rite: the ritual signing of the cross. Here the candidate makes the sign of the cross upon his/ her own forehead as a prophylactic against demons, or over objects (food, doorposts, etc.). The sign of the cross makes the demons flee, but only does so because the one making it has been sealed by the Holy Spirit through baptism and thus receives divine power: this power is, therefore, a fruit of baptism. This is the case in *Cat.* 4.14:

> Therefore let us not be ashamed of the cross of Christ; if someone else hides it, you seal yourself visibly upon the forehead, so that the devils, seeing the sign of the King, flee far away trembling. Make this sign when eating and drinking, when sitting, when lying down, when getting up, when speaking, when walking about; in general, at every act. (*PG* 33:472)

He tells them, 'for when you are about to dispute with unbelievers concerning the cross of Christ, proceed (by making) the sign of the cross of Christ with your hand, and the opponent will be silenced' (*Cat.* 13.22; *PG* 33:800). And more convincingly at 13.36:

> So let us not be ashamed to confess the one who was crucified. Let us make the cross openly on our forehead, as a seal, and at every moment: over the bread we eat, over the cups we drink; at our comings and goings; before sleep, when lying down and rising; when travelling or being still. (*PG* 33:816)

The sealing is not an action of a minister, bestowed either by a particular liturgical element (water, oil, the imposition of hands), nor is it an act reserved for the bishop (e.g. chrismation, confirmation, etc.). He tells them:

> Approach then the minister of baptism; not approaching the face of

the one you see before you, but remember the Holy Spirit of whom we now speak. For he is ready and present to seal your soul; and he will give you a seal at which devils tremble, that is heavenly and divine ... . (*Cat.* 17.35; *PG* 33:1009)

This review of Cyril's understanding of the 'seal' as that given by and for the Holy Spirit and simultaneously with the immersion, and no other liturgical act, demonstrates that in *Cats* we do not need to look for a chrismation for the bestowal of the Spirit through the physical actions of the oil and the minister such as we find in *MC* 3.

The Immersion

Theologically, the immersion is the central action of the rite by which the various effects of baptism are conveyed to the candidate. We have noted already how he connects sealing with the immersion to the extent that the presence of other sacramental rituals in this rite are in doubt. However, despite Cyril's concentration on this ritual to the exclusion of all others, he actually tells us very little about its conduct, and again we are reliant upon inference and what we have termed 'negative evidence'. Our investigation of the water rite requires three *foci*: the nature of the water; the manner of its administration; the ritual words.

For Cyril, the baptismal water is not 'ordinary water', but has clearly been consecrated:

Do not consider the water to be for an ordinary washing, but consider the spiritual grace being given with the water. For just as that which is offered at the altars, although ordinary in nature becomes defiled by the invocation of the idols; so too in the opposite way, ordinary water which receives the invocation of the Holy Spirit, and of Christ and the Father gains a new sanctifying power. (3.4; *PG* 33:429–430)

From this we might understand that the water has been blessed using a Trinitarian formula, either on its own or as the significant part of a consecratory prayer. We should note, though, that he gives two other possibilities. In *Procat.* 15, the water is, unusually, described as 'Christ-bearing': by entering the 'Christ-bearing waters', the candidates receive the name of Christ. In *Cats*, though, Cyril never speaks of the water in these terms despite the Jordan event being his preferred biblical narrative. Cyril's constantly connects the water with the Holy Spirit, thus in 3.4 'Therefore, when you are about to descend into the water, do not consider the ordinary water but receive salvation by power of the Holy Spirit'. Of course, a Trinitarian prayer over the water does not preclude these Christological and Pneumatological understandings of the immersion.

Cyril indicates that the candidates will be completely immersed in the water, and thus it is unlikely that water was poured over them. If the font discovered by Tinelli at the Holy Sepulchre complex is indeed that which Cyril's candidates used, then the dimensions would permit the candidate to stand in water above his knees and to be immersed by dipping or being pushed down.[25] Cyril says that they will 'enter the water' (3.4); they will 'go down into the water' (3.12). More explicitly, though, in his discussion of Pentecost, he says,

> ... for just as he who is covered by the waters and is baptized, is surrounded on all sides by water; so they were completely baptized by the Spirit. But the water flows only around the outside, whereas the Spirit baptizes entirely the soul within. (17.14; *PG* 33:985).

For the connection to be made between the Spirit surrounding the apostles and the water surrounding the candidates at baptism, Cyril must mean that they will be fully immersed. We are minded then to discount Cyril's statement in 3.16 about 'sprinkling' or 'pouring' water: 'The Lord will wash away the dirt from his sons and daughters ... He will sprinkle clean water upon you and you will be cleansed from your

---

[25] C. Tinelli, 'Il battistero del S. Sepolchro in Gerusalemme' in *Liber Annus* 23 (1973), pp. 95–104.

sins', (*PG* 33:448) which is, in any case, a paraphrase of Ezekiel 36.25.[26]

What of the words which accompanied the immersion? Cyril refers to 'invocations' over the water and/or the candidates. In 3.3, as we have seen above, the invocation of the Trinity effects a change in the element of water, and only secondarily in the candidate, and thus we have concluded that here Cyril means the consecration of the water. But in 3.12, he again mentions an 'invocation', which this time does affect the candidate:

> For you descend into the water carrying your sins; but the invocation of grace, having sealed your soul, does not permit you to be subdued by the terrifying dragon. (*PG* 33:441–444).

That the candidates' souls are sealed by an invocation makes it highly unlikely that they were subject to the interrogation mentioned in *MC* 2. We would expect the rite to have used a Trinitarian formula, but only once does Cyril cite or allude to the dominical command of Matthew 28.19: in 16.4, in a warning against separating the Spirit of the Old Testament from the Spirit in the New, he says,

> since that offends against the Holy Spirit herself, who is honoured with the Father and Son and is together in the Holy Trinity at the time of baptism. For the only-begotten Son of God said clearly to the apostles, 'Go out, make disciples of all people, baptizing them in the name of the Father and of the Son and of the Holy Spirit'. (*PG* 33:937)

And again in 16.19: 'The Holy Spirit ... is truly worthy of honour, and it is right that we are baptized into Father, Son and Holy Spirit' (*PG* 33:945). That this rite contained a Trinitarian baptismal formula is unremarkable, but there is more than one way of ritualizing these words, and this is what Cyril does not tell us. In *MC* 2, an immersion follows an assent to faith

---

[26] And again in *Cat.* 16.10 he paraphrases the same passage from Ezekiel.

in each member of the Trinity spread over the three immersions; in *Cats* there is no mention of assigning one immersion to each Person of the Trinity despite Cyril's frequent discussion of the Trinity and Unity of God. Nor do we know if the formula was recited as 'I baptize you in the name of ...', or 'N. is baptized in the name of ...' (preferred by Chrysostom).[27]

Anointing

So far we have found no evidence that the liturgy of baptism presumed by *Cats* has any anointing, which would make it most unusual. Distinctively, in places where one might expect Cyril to allude to oil or anointing, he never does so. Thus we see that, whereas in *MC* 3, the author plays on the words 'chrism' and 'christ' and then extrapolates this to the neophytes saying that by the anointing they too have become christs, in *Cats* this extrapolation is not attempted. Here 'christ' and *chreō* are related only to each other: 'He is called Christ, not having been anointed by human hands, but anointed eternally by the Father to his high priesthood over men' (*Cat.* 10.4; *PG* 33:664). This statement occurs in a section containing no liturgical information, direct or indirect, but a discourse on the titles applied to Christ. Later, 'Christ' is the determiner of (Christ's) priesthood: 'He is called ... Christ because of his priesthood' (10.11; *PG* 33:676). Now a connection is made with Aaron: Moses called Aaron 'christ', which denoted his priesthood, but there is no mention of an anointing (10.11), but in 10.14 Christ's priesthood is distinguished because he received it not by inheritance, 'nor was he anointed with manufactured oil' (*PG* 33:680). In 10.16, Cyril speaks of the generosity of Christ in giving his name to Christians, that name is received 'since we serve the Lord' (*PG* 33:681), and not because of an anointing, as in *MC*. And in *Cat.* 17 he again mentions the name 'Christians', but in connection with Antioch as the source of the name (Acts 11.26) and not as the result of a ritual. So whereas in *MC* 'Christ' and 'Christian' are explicitly consequent upon an anointing, in *Cats* no such connection is made.

---

[27] John Chrysostom, *Cat.* (Stav.) 2.26.

It would be highly unusual for a baptismal rite conducted in a major see in the presence of, if not the active participation of, the bishop to be without an anointing; elsewhere I showed that the evidence from other Palestinian sources indicated that those rites without anointings appear to be presbyteral and in desert locations.[28] But, as neither our investigation of 'seal' nor that into 'Christ', 'Christian' and *chreō*, provide any clear indication of the use of oil, the only path left open to us is speculation. Cyril, as we have noted, pours his entire theology of baptism into the font; there is no space in his interpretation for any other ritual. It would seem, then, that were there to have been an anointing, it carried no sacramental meaning, and may even have had no initiatory function. It was customary in the Graeco-Roman world for bathing to be preceded by a functional application of oil to the body, which was carried over into Christian liturgy. Thus, we suggest (speculate) that unconsecrated oil was applied to the candidates' bodies before the immersion following this custom; only later in the Jerusalem rite, as shown by *MC*, did oil receive the specific functions of exorcism and the bestowal of the Spirit. This would not be unusual and is the pattern attested by Chrysostom for Antioch.

The Imposition of Hands

Whether there was an imposition of hands depends in large part upon whether there was a ritual for the bestowal of the Holy Spirit additional to the immersion and, if so, whether this was administered by a post-immersion anointing or the imposition of hands. The ambiguity here is Cyril's. In this section on the Holy Spirit he comments,

> under Moses the Spirit was given by the imposition of hands; Peter also gave the Spirit through the imposition of hands; and upon you who are about to be baptized grace shall come; but I will

---

[28] See my, *Baptism in Early Byzantine Palestine 325–451* (Alcuin/GROW Liturgical Study 43; Cambridge, 1999).

not tell you how, as I will not anticipate the appropriate moment. (16.26; *PG* 33:956)

Does he mean that the Spirit is given by the imposition of hands, or that it is given by another ritual about which he will be silent? Again when speaking of the Ascension and Pentecost, he says,

> but Christ granted to his own disciples such enjoyment of the grace of the Holy Spirit, not just having it for themselves, but by the imposition of their hands (they) bestowed the communion of (the Spirit) on those who believed. (14.25; *PG* 33:857–860)

The section in which the latter occurs is an exposition of relevant scriptural passages and so the connection between the ritual and the Holy Spirit is likely to be as a consequence of that and not an allusion to the baptismal liturgy.

A conclusion in favour of an imposition of hands by which the Holy Spirit is ritually given is seriously weakened by Cyril's repeated assertions that the Holy Spirit is received in the water. Thus if there was a hand-laying, and we find the references insubstantial, then it was highly unlikely to have been related to the gift of the Spirit.

The Transitional Rituals

Elsewhere I have used the term 'transitional rituals' to denote those rituals preceding the Eucharist which demonstrate that the candidate has been initiated and are not initiatory in themselves; that is, they indicate the candidate's new status.[29] Such rituals may include post-immersion anointing, the imposition of hands, recitation of the Lord's Prayer or other prayers, processions into church with psalmody and/or candles and, of course, the putting on of a white robe.

---

[29] *The Baptismal Liturgy of Jerusalem*, pp. 120–121.

The evidence for the white robe is ambiguous. Cyril may allude to it in a passage interpreting the parable of the sheep and goats:

> So also, presently, when you have been cleansed of your sins, your actions will be as clean wool, your robe remains unsullied ... The sheep will be known by their external appearance. (*Cat.* 15.25; *PG* 33:908)

Shortly afterwards, though, he makes it clear that the robe in question is spiritual: 'Put on an incorruptible garment, shining with good works' (15.26; *PG* 33:908). Many have interpreted Egeria's reference to the newly baptized being clothed as an indication of a white robe, but, by *uiesti*, she may simply mean getting dressed after having stripped to enter the font (*It.Eg.* 38.1). *MC* 4.8 does contain a stronger allusion to the robe, but the passage is heavy with metaphor and is not conclusive. There may well have been a procession into church of the newly baptized for the Eucharist. Cyril tells them in *Cat.* 18.32 that they will be expected to proceed in 'reverence and order ... to the holy altar' for the Eucharist. Egeria, too, tells us:

> As soon as the *infants* have been baptized and clothed, and left the font, they are led with the bishop straight to the Anastasis. The bishop goes into the railed area and after one hymn says a prayer for them. Then he returns with them to the church, where all the people are keeping the vigil in the usual way. (*It.Eg.* 38.1)[30]

Elsewhere we have cast some doubt about the peregrinations of the bishop and neophytes, but we can at least be sure that their entry into church would have been noted by Egeria, who was a member of the congregation.[31]

---

[30] Wilkinson, p. 157.
[31] *The Baptismal Liturgy of Jerusalem*, p. 121–122.

A Summary Conclusion

We concluded our discussion of the ritual structure of the rite with a list of possible liturgical units, remarking that the notices of future instructions contained an ambiguity about the presence and number of post-immersion rituals which enabled 'sharing in the name' and 'sealing'. Our investigation of the individual units from the evidence of *Cats* has revealed this revised structure and content of the rite:

Summons to baptistery

The Pre-Immersion Rituals
A confession of sin possibly concluded by some sort of exorcistic ritual
A profession of faith, of unknown content but not the creed
A pre-immersion anointing with no liturgical or sacramental function

The Immersion
A consecration of the font with a Trinitarian formula
A complete immersion of the candidate with the recitation of a
Trinitarian formula of uncertain format
This effects the sealing of the candidate and the 'sharing in the name'

Post-Immersion Rituals
No anointing or imposition of hands

Transitional Rituals
Weak evidence for the white robe
A procession into church
Eucharist

From *Cats* to *MC*

If one compares the liturgy of baptism in *Cats,* presented above, with that of *MC,* one notes very significant differences in the ritual sequence of the rite as a whole, in the conduct of each liturgical unit and the theology applied to each. How liturgies change is a key methodological issue in liturgical studies, and one possible response is that a see or region becomes influenced by a source or practice which is considered more authoritative than its own. This, of course, is the purpose of the *Letter of Macarius* and the reason for its preservation in the Armenian tradition. That letter tells us that Jerusalem practice was to be preferred to their own traditions, and we can see this in relation to other liturgical practices and other regions: the liturgical year is a key example, and more recently I have added the anaphoral Benedictus to the list of Jerusalem's liturgical exports.[32] In the latter half of the fourth century, though, the evidence would point to Jerusalem importing liturgical practices, and I concluded my book with these words:

> It has become apparent that the 2 sources which lie closest to *MC*, both theologically and structurally, would appear to be those 'derived' from *AT*: *CH* and *AC*. If *AT*, as reconstructed, lies behind *CH* and *AC*, then the manner in which these 2 texts have interpreted their source is quite distinctive. It is possible, we suggest, that *MC* might be a hagiopolite interpretation of whatever source(s) – possibly even a version of *AT* – which lies behind the common sequence in *CH* and *AC*.[33]

It is of course not possible to say precisely the form in which the *Apostolic Tradition* was received in Jerusalem, given that the *Canons of Hippolytus* and the *Apostolic Constitutions,* for example, show differences from the Latin version, such that apostolic injunctions could be subject to editorial and regional preferences. We do not expect, therefore, to identify a single version of *AT* behind *MC*, but rather we will show how key liturgical features of the baptismal liturgy in *AT* and *CH* are evident in the Jerusalem rite of *MC*, but not in the rite presumed by *Cats*.

---

[32] See my 'The Origin of the Anaphoral Benedictus' in *Journal of Theological Studies* 60 (2009), pp. 193–211.

[33] *The Baptismal Liturgy of Jerusalem*, p. 138. *CH* is the *Canons of Hippolytus*; *AC* the *Apostolic Constitutions.*

The Jerusalem sources present us with a shift *from* a confession of sins followed by an exorcistic ritual *to* an explicit formula for the renunciation of Satan made in a westward-facing direction with an exorcistic anointing following the adherence. *MC* demonstrates here a clear affinity with *AT* 21 and *CH* 19: not only is the renunciation accomplished with the same orientation and with a similar formula, it is followed immediately by an anointing with exorcized oil.

The evidence for a change to the profession of faith is less marked: *Cats* may well have simply had a Trinitarian formula similar to that of *MC* ('I believe in the Father and in the Son and in the Holy Spirit and in the baptism of repentance'), or indeed have had an interrogation such as that occurring in the font. The ritual turning east in *MC* is also found in *CH* 19, but with a slightly different formula, 'I believe, and I submit myself to you and all your service, O Father, Son and Holy Spirit'.[34]

The pre-immersion anointing in *MC* is exorcistic, and we have suggested that there may be evidence for the confession of sins in *Cats* to have been followed by an exorcistic ritual and, more tentatively, that the rite might have had a non-liturgical anointing; we might posit therefore that this original exorcistic motif in *Cats* was retained and transferred to the pre-immersion anointing when the renunciation and adherence units were modified. Exorcistic oil is used in *AT* 21 and *CH* 19.

The immersion in *Cats* is conducted with a Trinitarian formula and not with an interrogation of faith, such as we find in *MC* 2, *AT* 21 and *CH* 19.

Cats appears to be without any post-immersion or transitional rituals, but *MC* 3 provides evidence for a post-immersion anointing with chrism for the gift of the Holy Spirit, with the oil being applied to specific locations (forehead, ears, nose, breast); *AT* and *CH* also apply oil 'of thanksgiving' to some of these specific locations but without the sacramental function that we find in *MC*.

We propose that the Jerusalem rite of *MC* has borrowed from *AT* and

---

[34] P. Bradshaw and C. Bebawi, *The Canons of Hippolytus* (Alcuin/GROW Liturgical Study 2; Nottingham, 1987), p. 22.

its derivatives in the following manner:

> The adoption of the interrogation in the font supplanted a Trinitarian formula, but the latter was retained as the formula for the adherence. The anointing before immersion copies *AT* in meaning and position; it was traditional in Jerusalem although in MC it is separated from the renunciation to which it belongs (as in *AT* and for 'ritual coherence'). The statement of renunciation of Satan replaces a confession of sins and the westward orientation of *AT* (*CH*, etc.) is adopted; but the manner of reciting the traditional profession of faith was altered to conform ritually with the renunciation following the pattern in *CH*.
>
> Jerusalem introduced a post-immersion anointing with chrism applied to specific locations again following the pattern of *AT* 21 and *CH* 19.

Conclusion

Although the evidence for the rite of baptism which concluded *Cats* is not at all complete and is in many ways elusive and inconclusive, there is sufficient for us to have attempted a credible reconstruction. This more detailed study of *Cats* combined with my earlier work on *MC* indicates the quite radical way in which Jerusalem transformed its baptismal liturgy theologically, structurally and ritually. We find that these changes are so fundamental that they cannot be due to any 'natural evolution' of the existing rite, and that they are caused by the adoption of another authoritative liturgical model. The model which most closely fits the baptismal liturgy of *MC* is the *Apostolic Tradition* in its various forms.